Dover Castle

Jonathan Coad

Introduction

The royal castle of Dover, dramatically sited above the cliffs overlooking the English Channel, is one of the most famous fortresses in north-west Europe. It has seen unbroken active service for over nine centuries, from the time of the Norman Conquest through to the Second World War and beyond. The castle has been attacked by medieval siege engines and cross-Channel guns. It has been visited by kings, queens, emperors and statesmen, and has been home to tens of thousands of soldiers.

Above: On 28 August 1940 during the Battle of Britain, Prime Minister Winston Churchill watches an air battle from the cliff tunnels

Facing page: Dover Castle from the sea, dominating the White Cliffs and the Straits of Dover

William the Conqueror constructed a castle at Dover following the battle of Hastings in 1066. It is likely that there was already an Iron Age hillfort here, and that the early castle was built within its earthworks, to control the town and port of Dover. However, its long-term importance has been as a frontier fortress, guarding the nearest landing point to mainland Europe.

Between 1170 and 1250, successive kings rebuilt and extended the castle, transforming it into the impressive fortress that we see today. In 1216 it withstood one of the greatest of English medieval sieges. From the 13th century to the early 18th century, the lords warden of the Cinque Ports made it their residence and headquarters; and from the 1740s onwards, the medieval banks and ditches were reshaped as the castle was modernized and adapted for artillery warfare. In the Second World War – almost uniquely for a castle – anti-aircraft guns became its main armament, and a crucial command-centre lay beneath the fortress in a network of underground tunnels, immune from bombing. In 1940, the castle was the nerve centre for the Dunkirk evacuation, and it was provisioned to stand as a rock of resistance against the threatened tide of a German invasion of Britain. The underground tunnels were adapted in the 1960s to serve as a regional seat of government after a nuclear attack.

Tour

Dover Castle has evolved over nearly 950 years, and its defences have been adapted to meet the changing needs of warfare. It has played host to numerous monarchs and statesmen, from William the Conqueror and Henry II to Winston Churchill. The tour covers the Roman lighthouse and Saxon church, the keep, the medieval tunnels, the outer defences and the secret wartime tunnels.

FOLLOWING THE TOUR

The site can be explored by different periods: early history, which includes the Roman lighthouse and Saxon church; the medieval period, which focuses on the keep; the outer fortifications and battlement walks, which are medieval but were adapted in the 18th century; and the modern period, which includes the secret wartime tunnels and Admiralty Look-out. Visitors can choose to explore just one or two periods, or to follow the guidebook tour round the whole site.
The numbers beside the headings highlight key points on the tour and correspond with the small numbered plans in the margins.

■ ROMAN LIGHTHOUSE AND SAXON CHURCH

The oldest building here is the Roman *pharos* or lighthouse, one of the most unusual surviving structures from Roman Britain. It stands at the highest point inside the later castle and was probably built early in the second century AD when the Romans were developing the port of Dover. It was constructed as an octagonal tower using local flint and Roman bricks, but only its lowest four stages survive. Its rectangular interior had a series of timber-floored chambers; at the top there was probably a platform for some kind of brazier. The lighthouse keeper might have lived in or next to the tower, but no evidence of such occupation has ever been found. It seems likely that the lighthouse ceased to be used regularly after the Romans left in the early fifth century, but a 12th-century reference to a lighthouse keeper here suggests that it may then have again been in operation. Later its exterior was refaced, and between 1415 and 1437 Humphrey, duke of Gloucester, rebuilt the top as a bell-tower for the neighbouring church.

This lighthouse was originally matched by another whose foundations were carefully preserved by Georgian military engineers building Drop Redoubt on the Western Heights (see the map on page 49). Fires burning on the top of these would have acted as beacons for shipping across the Straits to the harbour in between. A third tower, the now-vanished Tour d'Odre near Boulogne, acted as a guide for traffic crossing to Gaul.

Close beside the lighthouse stands the church of St Mary-in-Castro, built around 1000 and the finest late-Saxon building still standing in Kent. The reasons for the church's location on this windswept chalk hill remain unclear. The most likely explanation is that it was built within a now-vanished late-Saxon *burgh*, or defensive enclosure. Such enclosures were widely constructed during the troubled years at the start of the 11th century. As at Old Sarum in Wiltshire [also managed by English Heritage], earthworks of an Iron Age hillfort could have been used, or more compact defences may have been erected within these. Some *burghs* developed as permanent settlements. Limited archaeological excavations here in the 1960s revealed part of an adjacent 11th-century cemetery, suggesting this was probably the case here.

Although heavily restored in the 19th century, St Mary-in-Castro's cruciform [cross-shaped] plan, thick outer walls and massive central tower arches are largely original, incorporating Roman tiles. However, the chancel and crossing vaults, the

Above: The outline of a contemporary lighthouse scratched on a Roman floor tile. The two lighthouses at Dover were probably similar
Left: The Roman lighthouse and the Saxon church of St Mary-in-Castro. The church was restored in the 19th century after falling into ruin

Facing page: Looking north to Peverell's Gate on the western side of the castle, showing the inner and outer curtain walls protecting the great keep

5

chancel windows and the north doorway of the nave are modifications of the late 12th century, probably the work of the masons constructing the chapels in Henry II's new keep. An original doorway high in the west wall indicates that the church was originally linked to the lighthouse, suggesting that its use as a bell-tower may predate its conversion in the 15th century.

By the early 18th century the church had fallen into ruins. During the Napoleonic Wars (1803–15) it was used as a fives court [a ball game similar to squash, but played with bats or the hands] and then a coal store. In 1862 as part of a campaign to improve the life of the British soldier, it was carefully restored as the garrison church by the architect Sir George Gilbert Scott. Later, in 1888 William Butterfield added the brick top to the tower and the mosaic decoration inside the nave.

South of the church and lighthouse there are fine views from the surrounding medieval bank, dating from about 1230, and from the remains of its curtain wall, added in 1256. Both overlie an earlier mid-11th-century earthwork. This may possibly be part of the castle that William the Conqueror is known to have constructed here in November 1066. Equally, it could have been

defences hastily thrown up by the townspeople after hearing of his landing at Pevensey a few weeks earlier. The present bank and wall originally linked to the eastern outer defences near Pencester's Tower and ran westwards to Peverell's Tower via Colton's Gate. The wall was demolished in 1772 but Colton's Gate, built by King John, and the curtain wall beyond it, give an impression of the height of the missing sections. North of the church are the earthworks of Four-Gun Battery, constructed in 1756. The adjacent church hall was built a century later as the schoolroom for the children of the garrison.

2 INNER BAILEY

Palace Gate marks the entrance to the inner bailey. The grassy mound south of the gate once housed a steam pump for the great well dug in the 1790s. The inner bailey walls, built by Henry II in the 1180s, are punctuated by 14 projecting rectangular wall towers, enabling defenders to use flanking fire to prevent an enemy approaching the main curtain walls. The two gateways are well protected between pairs of towers, the earliest English examples of such planning. Both gateways had outer defence works, or barbicans, but only the northern one survives. Its outer barbican

Below: An engraving by the Buck brothers of the ruins of the church of St Mary-in-Castro and the Roman lighthouse in the early 18th century

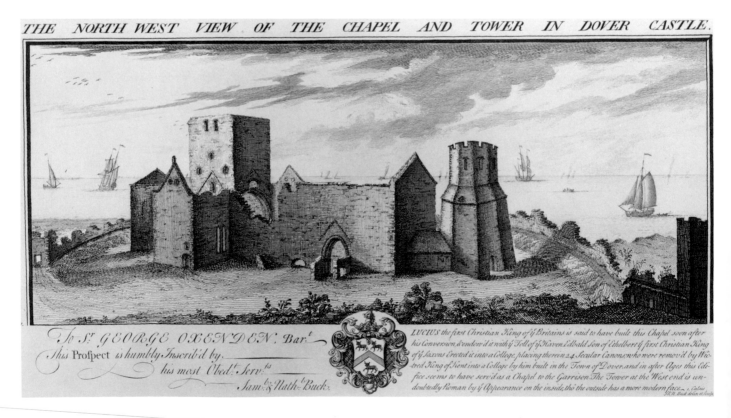

THE NORTH WEST VIEW OF THE CHAPEL AND TOWER IN DOVER CASTLE.

To S.ʳ GEORGE OXENDEN. Barᵗ
This Prospect is humbly Inscrib'd by
his most Obedᵗ Servᵗˢ
Samˡ & Nathˡ Buck.

LUCIUS the first Christian King of ỹ Britains is said to have built this Chapel soon after his Conversion, & endow'd it with ỹ Toll of ỹ Haven, Eldbald Son of Ethelbert ỹ first Christian King of ỹ Saxons Erected it into a College, placing therein 24 Secular Canons, who were remov'd by Wictred King of Kent into a College by him built in the Town of Dover, and in after Ages this Edifice seems to have serv'd as a Chapel to the Garrison. The Tower at the West end is undoubtedly Roman by ỹ Appearance on the inside, tho' the outside has a more modern face. ₁ Colina

Left: *The keep and King's Gate from the north. The deliberately off-set entrance to the barbican helped protect the gate from assault*

Below: *A reconstruction of life in a Georgian barracks similar to those in Keep Yard. British soldiers then slept two to a bed; married men and their wives draped hangings round their beds for a modicum of privacy*

gateway is deliberately not aligned with the inner gateway, to blunt the rush of any attacking force. The wall towers, which have been extensively refaced, were reduced in height at the end of the 18th century to improve fields of fire for artillery. In the 1850s, military engineers remodelled the wall-walks and parapets and modified the two gateways with counter-balanced lifting bridges.

The inner bailey was the busy hub of castle life, witnessing comings and goings of monarchs and courtiers, ambassadors, royal messengers, soldiers and prisoners, tradesmen and merchants. Until the siege of 1216, when the north gateway was blocked, most visitors arrived at the north gateway of the castle, reaching the inner bailey through King's Gate. After the siege, people probably mostly came through Constable's Gate and Palace Gate.

From early on, buildings would have lined the curtain walls. Nearly all the existing buildings were constructed by the military engineer John Peter Desmaretz in the 1750s as barracks, making them some of the oldest in the country. Many of these incorporate fragments of earlier buildings, the most important of which is Arthur's Hall. This great hall, built for Henry III in 1240, provided the king with more modern and convenient

accommodation than was available in the keep. It was once linked to the keep by a covered passageway. The lower part of Arthur's Hall is still visible within the barracks on the eastern side of the inner bailey. The most recent building, now a café, was constructed in 1901 as a mobilization store for the royal garrison artillery reservists, who helped to man Dover's coastal guns in wartime.

CUTAWAY RECONSTRUCTION
OF THE KEEP IN ABOUT 1190

*A conjectural reconstruction
drawing of the furniture and
decoration of the keep during
a royal visit in about 1190.
Recent research suggests that
the roofs were deeply sunk
within the building*

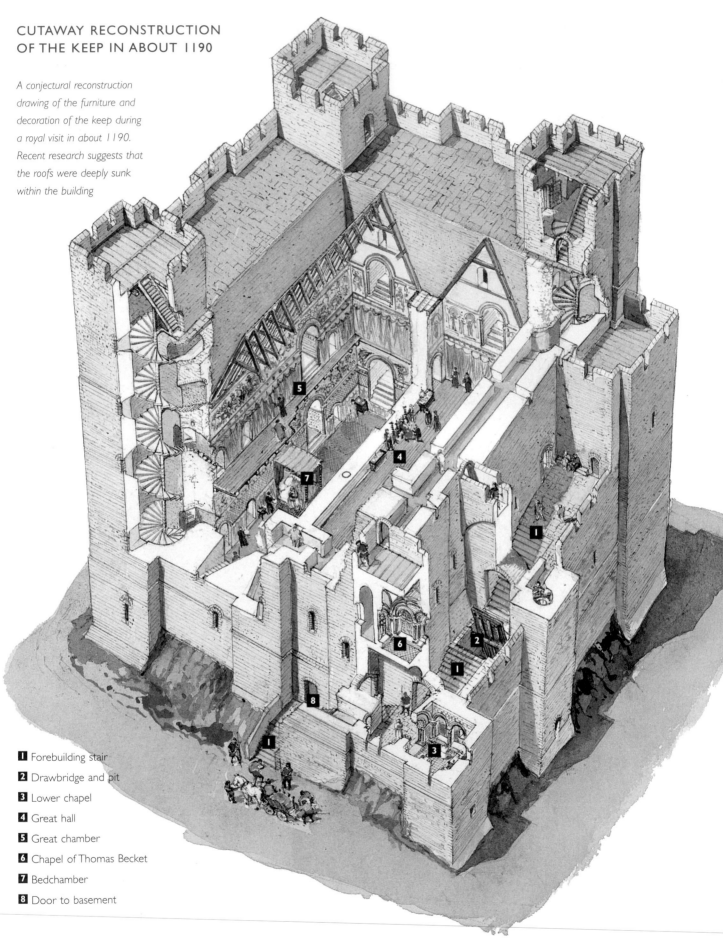

1 Forebuilding stair
2 Drawbridge and pit
3 Lower chapel
4 Great hall
5 Great chamber
6 Chapel of Thomas Becket
7 Bedchamber
8 Door to basement

▣ HENRY II'S KEEP

Dover keep was the last and most elaborate in the tradition of the huge rectangular royal keeps, begun in England the previous century with the Tower of London and Colchester. It was built over ten years from about 1180. It is an impressive building, and stands 25.3m high, with walls up to 6.4m thick in places. The ground floor was primarily used for storage, but the two floors above formed two pairs of magnificent great halls, divided by a full-height cross-wall. Linking these are two internal spiral staircases set within the walls diagonally opposite each other.

Like all royal keeps, it had multiple functions. Seen originally as an occasional residence or palace for the monarch and his court, it was also a lodging for important travellers waiting to cross to France, a storehouse and the ultimate stronghold during a siege.

Below: The north face of the keep

PLANS OF THE KEEP

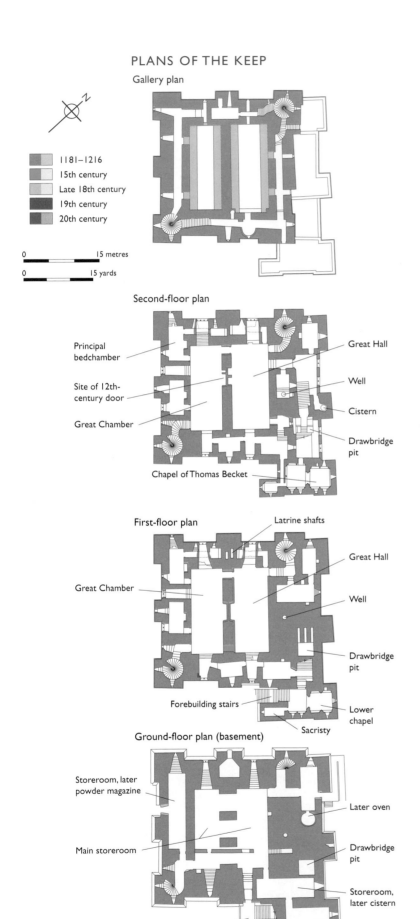

Gallery plan

1181–1216
15th century
Late 18th century
19th century
20th century

0   15 metres
0   15 yards

Second-floor plan

Principal bedchamber

Site of 12th-century door

Great Chamber

Chapel of Thomas Becket

Great Hall

Well

Cistern

Drawbridge pit

First-floor plan

Latrine shafts

Great Chamber

Forebuilding stairs

Sacristy

Great Hall

Well

Drawbridge pit

Lower chapel

Ground-floor plan (basement)

Storeroom, later powder magazine

Main storeroom

Forebuilding entrance

Later oven

Drawbridge pit

Storeroom, later cistern

From time to time, the keep was modernized, notably in the second half of the 15th century. In 1625 elaborate preparations made here to receive Charles I's bride, Henrietta Maria, did not impress the French and this marked the end of the keep's use as a royal lodging. Thereafter, it reverted to a military role: as prisoner-of-war accommodation in the early 18th century, then as barracks for troops. Late in the 1790s a new brick-vaulted roof was constructed as a platform for heavy guns. After that, the keep became a weapons and ammunition store and during the First World War searchlights were mounted on the roof against German air attacks. During the Second World War, it was used as military offices.

4 Forebuilding

The stairs in the forebuilding lead straight up to the second-floor state apartments, where the tour of the keep begins.

The forebuilding is the elaborately protected ceremonial entrance to the main second floor of the keep, its steps passing through two gate towers and over a drawbridge to a third tower dominating the top of the steps. Until the 15th century, the spaces between these towers were unroofed, allowing defenders to fire down on to any enemy on the steps.

Just above the existing steps is evidence of an earlier flight of stairs which did not turn through a right-angle as now before reaching the inner bailey. At the lowest landing an original doorway leads directly into the basement. Although very well protected, this would have been an unacceptable weakness in an earlier keep lacking concentric outer defences.

SECTION THROUGH THE KEEP

Within the first forebuilding tower is the lower of two richly decorated chapels, apparently always open to passers-by on the forebuilding steps. Adjacent is a vaulted sacristy for a priest. The steps pass a 15th-century doorway on the left before a modern timber bridge spans the medieval drawbridge pit to the second gate tower. This leads to the second-floor landing and a further guardroom. Outside this, marks on the wall are the ghosts of a stone bench, cunningly warmed by a chimney flue. On the left, the 12th-century doorway decorated with a moulded, round-headed arch and angle shafts with stiff foliated capitals is the ceremonial entrance to the keep.

5 Well Chamber

Left of the entrance passage in the immense thickness of the outer wall is the original well chamber. The well is dug through some 122m

First floor

4

Second floor

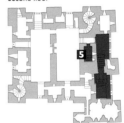

5

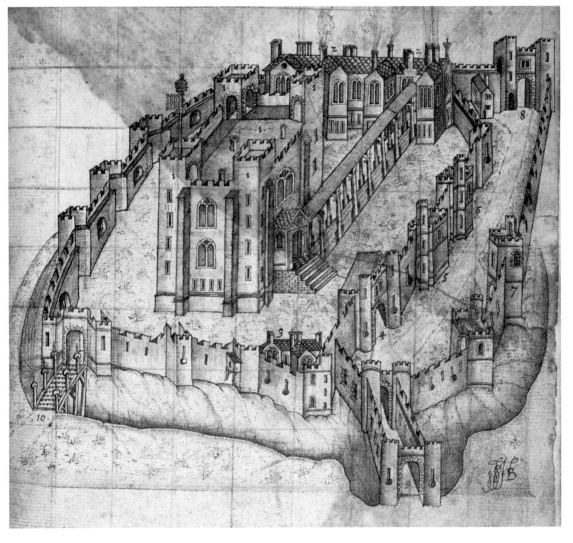

Above left: The 12th-century lower chapel in the keep forebuilding
Left: The keep and inner bailey from the west in 1626. John Bereblock's view shows the prominent corridor linking the keep to Arthur's Hall

Above: Arms and armour displayed in the great hall of the keep in the early 20th century

(400ft) of chalk to reach water. Without this, no garrison could withstand a lengthy siege. Here, the well was deliberately made accessible only at second-floor level in case the basement was captured. Remarkably, the keep originally had a piped water supply to the lower floors from the well chamber; the remains of two lead pipes survive left of the well-head.

6 State Apartments (Second Floor)

The entrance passage opens into the first of two nearly identical-sized halls, used on occasion as state apartments. The original height of these rooms is uncertain, following the insertion of brick vaults in the 1790s, which replaced a pair of shallow timber roofs. However, recent research suggests that the original 12th-century roofs may

Second floor

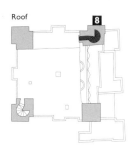

Roof

one has its own latrine, suggesting that this set of rooms was perhaps designed as sleeping quarters for the monarch during visits.

A room within the southern wall, linked to the high ends of the great hall and great chamber, may originally have been a servery for final food preparation. Its 18th-century western doorway may replace an earlier one that allowed a direct route from the king's private apartments to the upper chapel.

7 Chapel of Thomas Becket

The upper chapel is in the first tower over the forebuilding steps immediately above the lower chapel. Next to it is a little sacristy for the priest, still with its original stone benches. The chapel itself is a church in miniature, with a tiny nave and chancel. As with the lower chapel, both sacristy and chapel are notable for the richness of their mouldings: the vault ribs with dog-tooth ornament, the arcaded walls, the shafts and columns with foliated capitals and the chancel arch enriched with chevron decoration. These closely match contemporary work at Canterbury Cathedral, indicating that the same masons worked on both major projects. Later the chapel was dedicated to Thomas Becket, the archbishop murdered in Canterbury Cathedral by four of Henry II's knights, a few years before the king began his great reconstruction of Dover.

have been substantially lower, screened by the full height of the outer walls of the keep.

The present windows are 15th-century replacements, probably contemporary with the fireplaces and the repositioned doorway linking the halls. Some of the fireplaces, such as the one in the bedchamber, are decorated with Edward IV's badge of the *rose en soleil* (an open rose); the blocked original doorway is to the left of the fireplace in the great chamber. The timber floors may be 18th-century.

There are two main rooms on the second floor: the great hall and the great chamber. The first of these rooms is the great hall, where most people would have lived, eaten and slept. It was also the gathering place for those awaiting audience with the king in the adjacent great chamber. Here the king would have held court, conferred with his chief officials, issued instructions, heard petitions and dispensed justice. These rooms would have been richly furnished with wall-hangings; they were also the setting for state events, entertainments and banquets.

The need to accommodate what was in effect a small medieval royal palace here led to some complicated planning. Opening off the great hall and great chamber are smaller rooms within the thickness of the outer walls. A number are latrines for common use. Only the monarch would normally have had a measure of privacy. Off the great chamber are two small rooms; each has a fireplace, modernized in the 15th century, and

Above left: This richly furnished interior suggests how the state apartments in the keep may have looked when the king was in residence. Edward IV, portrayed here, modernized Dover keep in the 15th century

Left: The chapel of Thomas Becket. Its richly decorated stonework is derived from contemporary work at Canterbury Cathedral

The 1265 Siege

The widowed countess hired 29 archers and prepared to hold out

In July 1263 Dover Castle surrendered to Simon de Montfort, earl of Leicester and leader of the opposition to Henry III during the barons' war. Simon's son Henry became constable. After the king's defeat at the battle of Lewes in May 1264, the future Edward I was briefly held prisoner here.

In June 1265, Simon's wife Eleanor de Montfort, her three-year-old daughter Eleanor and supporters arrived at Dover to rally support for the barons' cause. But on 4 August 1265 the baronial forces led by Simon were soundly defeated at the battle of Evesham and Simon and his son Henry were both killed. At Dover, the widowed countess hired 29 archers and prepared to hold out. Events then took a dramatic turn when 14 royalist knights – prisoners in the keep – seized control with the aid of some of the garrison. The doors to the keep were barricaded and Eleanor's men were unable to break in. When news reached London, Prince Edward hastily collected forces and laid siege to the castle. A contemporary account recorded that, 'those within the tower [the keep] were well provisioned... The garrison, who were being indefatigably attacked from both within and without, could not continue to resist this divided assault.' The countess, sister of Henry III, surrendered to her nephew Prince Edward who treated her courteously and sent her into exile. Damage to the castle appears to have been minimal and the strength of Henry II's keep was vividly demonstrated.

Right: An attack on a medieval castle using scaling ladders

Facing page: The east side of the keep with the three towers of the forebuilding. Beyond stand the mid-18th-century army barracks

8 Roof

A doorway beside the entrance to the great hall leads to the spiral staircase to the roof. On the way up is a narrow wall passage in the thickness of the outer walls. The insertion of the brick vaults in 1799 has obscured its original purpose. If the first roofs were set lower, this passage would have been a kind of gallery running round at eaves level within the upper walls of the keep, screening the roofs. With later higher roofs, such as existed at least by the 18th century, the passage's main use was to overlook the upper halls, providing some additional ventilation and light.

The magnificent views from the roof of the keep reveal the huge extent of the castle's defences as well as some of the other fortifications that once ringed Dover. On the hill west of the town are the immense earthworks of Western Heights (see the map on page 49). North-east of the castle, beyond the former 20th-century barracks, is Fort Burgoyne, begun in 1860. Remains of the gun positions installed on the keep roof in about 1800 remain along the east side. Most of the crenellations are restorations of the early 1930s. The central area of the roof once supported a huge cast-iron water tank installed here in 1898, sweeping away earlier chimney stacks.

9 First Floor

The spiral stairs from the roof go back down to the first floor. Here, the layout mirrors the state apartments above. There is the same sequence of great hall and great chamber, with extra rooms within the thickness of the outer walls. Decorative detail here is notably less elaborate and this floor has no private chapel. Although it lacks the grand approach enjoyed by the second floor, the resultant greater security here suggests that this level had an important, if perhaps less formal, use.

The heavy timber framing partly lining the walls of the great hall dates from the 13th century, when it was added presumably to strengthen the floor above. It was largely encased in brick during the 15th century. On this floor a doorway off the north-east spiral stair leads to two fine barrel-vaulted rooms constructed immediately below the upper landing and forebuilding guardroom. These may have been used by minor officials.

10 Basement

A doorway altered in the 18th century leads to the stairs from the keep. In one wall of the lobby at the bottom is a 15th-century oven. This was almost certainly for bread-making and is the only evidence we have for any cooking facilities within the keep. It seems most likely that there was always a separate, detached kitchen in the south-east corner of the inner bailey, suggesting that medieval meals in the keep can rarely have been served very hot. The external door by the oven is an 18th-century insertion, probably dating from the keep's use as barracks. The basement today contains an exhibition, accessed from outside the keep. It was once the principal storeroom of the castle, and for much of its time it was probably mostly empty. But when the castle was provisioned for war it would have held food and munitions: sacks of corn, dried foodstuffs, barrels of ale, firewood, arrows, long bows and cross-bows, as well as (probably dismantled) stone-throwing engines and their missiles. Without such resources – the modern equivalents of which were last stockpiled in the castle as recently as June 1940 – no garrison could hope to withstand a siege.

The immense solidity of the keep is readily apparent at this level, where the two main rooms, linked by three arches in the cross-wall, are smaller because of the greater thickness of the outer walls. On the south side is one of the few original windows not replaced in the 15th century. Probably contemporary with the later windows are the remains of the cross-wall at the southern end. This would have subdivided the storage space, perhaps for better security. The well-protected southern entrance with its series of barred doors was used as the main entrance for stores.

First floor

Basement

◫ MEDIEVAL TUNNELS

The entrance to the medieval tunnels is at the foot of the spiral stairs beneath the stone bridge that once linked King's Barbican to the rampart behind the outer curtain.

These tunnels form part of an extraordinary defensive system first constructed by Hubert de Burgh after the siege of 1216. Throughout the siege, the French had concentrated assaults on the main gateway at the northern tip of the castle. This was Dover's most vulnerable point. Higher ground to the north gave the French the advantage of being able to direct their fire down on to the defenders while their miners dug beneath the fortifications. In 1216, Louis's troops succeeded in capturing the outer defences after miners had weakened the timber palisades (stockade). The miners then concentrated on the north gateway itself, eventually undermining its eastern tower. Only ferocious fighting by the garrison, led by Hubert

de Burgh, and the subsequent blocking of the ruined gateway with tree trunks, saved the castle.

Immediately after the siege, Hubert set about remedying the castle's structural weaknesses. A series of new defences was built, linked together by underground tunnels. A new and far more strongly protected gateway – Constable's Gate – was built on the western side of the castle. To augment this, and to allow defenders to sally out on both sides of the castle, Fitzwilliam Gate was constructed on the eastern side.

When these new gates were completed, the north gateway with its twin towers was blocked solid; these are now known as the Norfolk Towers. In front of these, the circular St John's Tower was constructed in the moat. On higher ground to the north, once occupied partly by the barbican, Hubert built a substantial defensible earthwork or spur. This seems to have been roughly oval-shaped with a curtain and possibly three towers from

Facing page: The communication tunnels constructed after the siege of 1216–17 to link the castle to the new northern defence-work or spur

Below: French forces assault the old north gate of the castle. A dramatic reconstruction of this critical moment during the siege of 1216–17

where defenders could pour fire on an enemy intent on attacking this end of the castle. The most ingenious element of the scheme was the link constructed mostly underground between the castle and this detached spur. This was designed to provide a protected line of communication for soldiers manning the spur, and to allow the garrison to gather unseen before launching a surprise sortie. A tunnel led from behind the Norfolk Towers to St John's Tower. From there, a drawbridge on its northern face led to a short tunnel within the chalk of the spur itself.

Although the spur was apparently abandoned and in ruins by the 16th century, Hubert's remarkable communications system seems to have survived partially intact until the end of the 18th century. Then a new generation of military engineers sought to strengthen the northern end of the castle and improve the defences here. The medieval spur was remodelled to its present plan and considerably strengthened. As part of this work, the tunnels were substantially enlarged and further modernised in the 1850s. In their date and complexity they remain unique.

Right: The vaulted guardroom in the spur completed by 1804

Below: The arrow-shaped redan built on the spur in the 1790s to mount additional artillery. In the moat is St John's Tower, its parapets modified for musketry in the 1750s. Beyond is the original north gate, blocked after the siege of 1216–17 and now part of the Norfolk Towers

The spiral stairs leading down to the brick-lined tunnel were constructed by the military engineer William Twiss in the 1790s. Twiss cut short the north end of the bridge that once linked King's Barbican to the earth rampart behind the outer curtain to make way for the existing casemated barracks. The brick tunnel links to the steeply sloping communications passage dug in the chalk by Hubert de Burgh's miners in the 1220s. A little further down, this passage cuts through a rough-hewn cross-gallery which lies at a slightly higher level. This may be one of the counter-mining tunnels dug by the garrison in the hope of intercepting the French miners in 1216. A little beyond this, an iron grating in the floor covers a vertical shaft to a still deeper tunnel of early 19th-century date. This provided a lower tier of communication to the outer defences and allowed for mining the Deal road.

The medieval tunnel emerges through the castle bank into a short covered passage to a tall entrance in the southern side of St John's Tower in the middle of the moat. From the parapets of this tower, which were remodelled for riflemen in the 1750s, it was possible to command the spur, while from its two sallyports on the ground floor defenders could sortie into the moat.

On the northern side of the tower, the medieval doorway, protected by a portcullis, once led to a drawbridge to a covered way into the spur itself. These were replaced by the existing two-storey brick caponier (a protected communication way), designed and largely completed by Georgian military engineers by 1804,

block access between the lower level and the spur should the latter be captured. The only way into the spur from the castle is through this lower level of the caponier, reached by the timber stair in St John's Tower. Down here the evidence for the medieval drawbridge can be seen. At the end of this level a spiral stair, covered by firing loops from the upper floor, leads back up to the northern section of the medieval tunnel within the spur itself. Here, the tunnel divides into three passages completed in the 1230s, two of which are now blocked. The vaulting in two of these shows that they originally continued upwards, giving the garrison protected access to all parts of this medieval northern defence work.

The one surviving medieval passage was adapted to link with Napoleonic guardrooms protecting a doorway leading out to the rear of the spur. This guardroom is notable for its firing loops and for the extraordinary sequence of lever-controlled doors that allowed the guards to control access. If necessary they could divert the enemy into a walled enclosure, where they could be shot at from above.

Left: The ingenious system of iron levers in the spur guardroom that controls the exit doors
Below: The upper floor of the caponier linking the spur, as reconstructed at the end of the 18th century. Carronades, which fired heavy shot a short distance, were ideal weapons for covering the moat

but modified in the 1850s. In many ways, the ingenuity of these later engineers is even more remarkable than that of their medieval predecessors. Along the caponier, firing loops on both sides allowed defenders to sweep the moat with carronades (large-bore, short-range naval guns) and muskets. At the far end of the upper floor is a falling door that could be dropped to

Brigadier-General William Twiss

Modernizing Dover's defences in the Napoleonic wars was the climax of William Twiss's career. His work demonstrates the wide variety of tasks and opportunities available for a Royal Engineer. By the end of the 18th century, the corps' responsibilities extended beyond fortifications and siege works. Twiss first served in the fortress towns of Portsmouth, Plymouth and Gibraltar, where he gained experience of naval works before being sent to America in 1776. There he organized moving some 500 boats to Lake Champlain, where he constructed a small dockyard. His road-making skills played a crucial part in the taking of Fort Ticonderoga. Captured at the battle of Saratoga, he was exchanged for American prisoners and sent to Canada, where he built another small naval base beside Lake Ontario. In 1779 he constructed the Coteau-du-Lac Canal, the first with locks in North America, an experience that proved useful later during construction of the Royal Military Canal on Romney Marsh. After serving as chief engineer in Canada, he returned to England and in 1792 was appointed commanding Royal Engineer for the southern military district. Fears of invasion prompted a huge increase in defence works and Twiss remained here, retiring in 1809. As well as work at the castle, Twiss extended the fortifications of Western Heights on the other side of Dover – the largest fortification project in Britain during the Napoleonic wars. Much of his work remains, including the unique Grand Shaft, its three concentric staircases within a pair of circular brick shafts linking the town to the fortress above. He had a major role in the design and location of the Martello Tower chain along the Kent and Sussex coasts and also rebuilt Fort Cumberland at Portsmouth. He also took part in the 1799 expedition to Holland, advising on the destruction of the Bruges canal. In 1802 he visited Ireland to report on its defences, while from 1794 to 1810 he was also Lieutenant-Governor of the Royal Military Academy.

Captured at the battle of Saratoga, he was exchanged for American prisoners and sent to Canada

Above: Portrait of William Twiss by Sir Thomas Lawrence

BATTLEMENTS WALK

There are stunning views of the castle and the surrounding areas from the circuit of the outer walls of the medieval castle (see plan on inside back cover). The eastern half of the walk starts by the entrance to the medieval tunnels and the western half by Canon's Gate, near the entrance to the secret wartime tunnels.

12 Eastern Route

The gun ramp immediately east of the entrance to the medieval tunnels leads to the rampart. Guns and their timber carriages were normally stored under cover until needed. The wide earth rampart to Avranches Tower was constructed in the 1750s by Desmaretz. Its width allowed space to deploy heavy guns and gave extra strength to the medieval walls to withstand bombardment. To give gunners a clear field of fire, the towers were also reduced in height, but the wall remains substantially as completed by Henry II and King John.

At the top of the ramp there is a good view of the northern end of the castle with its layers of defences. The northern outer entrance, blocked in the 1220s and now known as the Norfolk Towers, was remodelled again in about 1800, when Twiss added the brick casemated barracks. These barracks supported guns overlooking St John's Tower and the medieval spur, which was remodelled in the 1750s, when brick parapets were added. In its centre, the arrow-shaped brick redan was built in the 1790s, probably as a mortar position.

South of the gun ramp is Fitzwilliam Gate of the 1220s. Its grim, beak-shaped towers mirror the Norfolk Towers. Although lacking the formal grandeur of Constable's Gate, Fitzwilliam Gate also had accommodation over it, of which fragments remain. Originally a covered bridge crossed the outer moat to the gateway in the outer bank. During the Napoleonic Wars, military engineers rebuilt the bridge with a caponier beneath it, from where troops could fire along the moat. The present steps, gates and brick bridge parapets date from army alterations in the 1930s.

The road continues past Fitzwilliam Gate, below the formidable walls of the inner bailey. Ahead, on the skyline, are the menacing gun embrasures of Bell Battery, constructed in 1756. The path on the left leads to Avranches Tower. The castle plan shows the northern section of the eastern moat

Left: An early 19th-century view of the underground barracks in the cliffs
Below: Avranches Tower, a powerful polygonal structure, with a double row of arrowloops, built in the 1180s to control an angle in the eastern defences

overlapping the southern stretch at this point, suggesting that this may once have been the entrance to an Iron Age hillfort. Henry II's engineers overcame this potential weakness by constructing the powerful polygonal Avranches Tower and the adjacent stretch of curtain wall. Together, these have over 50 arrowloops in two tiers.

Georgian and Victorian military engineers further fortified this area. The narrow passage known as Avranches lower flank, leading to the site of Pencester Tower, is mostly late 18th-century. From it, Georgian infantry could fire over the moat and outer defences, while in casemates below gunners raked the moat with grapeshot.

South of Pencester Tower, the medieval moat was greatly enlarged and given brick walls in the 1790s by Twiss. Behind, the outer curtain wall was largely buried by the massive earth ramparts. Twiss also constructed the four great bastions beyond the outer moat: Horseshoe, Hudson's, East Arrow and East Demi-Bastion. These were sited to allow extra guns and mortars to cover the north-eastern hillside and to provide flanking fire along the eastern defences. A series of tunnels linked these to the castle.

A narrow tunnel past the remains of Pencester Tower leads to the ramparts at Bell Battery. From here the battlements walk runs along the ramparts nearly to the cliff edge. The gun emplacements here have original smooth-bore guns, some on

replica iron garrison or display carriages. At intervals are 19th-century 'expense' magazines, a number of which have been covered over for extra protection. These stored gunpowder for immediate use, until supplies could arrive from the castle's main powder magazines.

Further along, the four circular concrete bases were for anti-aircraft guns, installed during the Second World War – the last active weapons ever to be mounted at the castle. Towards the cliff top are two Second World War brick observation posts. Beyond the fence, the hexagonal brick and concrete structure at the end of the medieval curtain wall was part of a naval radar station, installed in 1943 to watch for enemy shipping in the Straits. Its information was relayed directly to the Admiralty headquarters in the cliff below. Nearby, steps lead down to the road, passing a powder magazine protected within the bank.

On the opposite side of the road lies the vast officers' new barracks, constructed between 1856 and 1858 to a design by the architect Anthony Salvin. It originally housed 45 bachelor officers of the Dover garrison and an officers' mess. Car parks to the rear occupy the sites of other 19th-century army buildings.

Above left: Gunners being trained in the 1850s. This photograph was probably taken at Woolwich Arsenal, but similar drill would have been a feature of garrison life at Dover

Above: Round shot. Early cannon balls were stone, but these were largely superseded by cast iron in the 16th century. By the 1850s new guns firing explosive shells had made such ammunition obsolete

Left: The officers' new barracks, constructed in the 1850s as part of a modernization of the garrison accommodation

Facing page: Bell Battery, constructed in 1756. The magazine building is a 19th-century addition

Right: The fire-control post in 1941. A drawing by the war artist Anthony Gross (1905–84)

Below: Admiral Sir Bertram Ramsay's statue on the cliff top above his underground headquarters, by Steve Melton

🔢 Admiralty Look-out

Throughout most of Dover Castle's military life, the impregnable cliff on its southern boundary needed no further defences. From the 16th century, guns were occasionally positioned here to allow plunging fire on hostile ships approaching the harbour from the east. However, development of more powerful ordnance in the mid-19th century, and a need to protect the expanding harbour, led to the first permanent gun batteries along the cliff edge. Between 1871 and 1874, East Demi-Bastion was re-equipped with two of the new rifled muzzle-loading guns, while Hospital Battery, Shot Yard Battery and Shoulder of Mutton Battery were constructed to mount a further 13 heavy weapons. By 1905, advances in centralized weapon control allowed conversion of the then obsolete Hospital Battery into a fire-control post, overseeing all the guns protecting the harbour. In 1914, the Admiralty port war signal station was built immediately above it, to control shipping movements within Dover harbour. These two installations, now known as Admiralty Look-out, played notable parts throughout the First and Second World Wars.

Admiralty Look-out stands on the cliff edge, distinguished by its tall naval signalling mast used for communicating with shipping. The reinforced concrete roof and the blast-walls to the rear were added in 1941 as protection from air attacks. A modern external stair leads to the roof from where there are spectacular views across the Straits to France.

The building below consists of the port war signal station of 1914, above the fire control post of 1905. The remains of Hospital Battery can be seen on either side, although much of the western part was buried in the 1960s, when a lift-shaft to the cliff tunnels was built during the Cold War. To the rear of Admiralty Look-out is the site of the 19th-century garrison hospital, after which the earlier battery was named.

West of Admiralty Look-out is Steve Melton's statue of Admiral Sir Bertram Ramsay, unveiled in November 2000. The bas-reliefs on the plinth, depicting the evacuation of Dunkirk in 1940 and the Normandy invasion of 1944 are by Duncan Scott. These commemorate Ramsay's key role in the organization of these two operations, the first of which he planned and directed from his naval headquarters in the cliffs below.

On the right of the road, a rectangular, stone-faced, windowless building with a steel door houses the 1960s lift to the regional seat of government, once housed in the tunnels below.

Next to it is a 19th-century double spiral staircase to the Georgian underground barracks. A little further down the road, a path on the left leads past railings marking the rear of Shot Yard Battery, where two heavy guns were once mounted. The emplacements can be seen through the trees. The magazine for ammunition is buried in the earthworks on the left. The flat-roofed brick building was built after the battery had become obsolete and was probably used for some form of wartime radio transmitting. To the right of the path is the circular top of one of the ventilation shafts, constructed in the 1790s for the underground barracks. Along the path, just near Canon's Gate, is the entrance to the secret wartime tunnels. Beyond this is the start of the western battlements walk.

Left: Shot Yard Battery photographed in the 1870s. The rear entrance to the cliff tunnels is in the right foreground
Below: The port war signal station and fire-control post on the cliff edge. The concrete roof was added in 1941 to protect against air raids

Above: Dover Castle from the west, about 1767. This painting by Arthur Nelson shows the western side of the medieval castle still largely unaltered and dominating the small town of Dover

Below: The regimental institute, built in 1868 and later enlarged, provided recreation and reading facilities for the Victorian garrison

14 Western Route

The development of the western outer defences of the castle largely mirrors those on the eastern side. The medieval walls were constructed in the first 30 years of the 13th century. They were extensively adapted for artillery by Twiss during the Revolutionary and Napoleonic wars at the end of

the 18th century. Here too, he reduced the medieval towers in height and backed the walls with earth ramparts. Compared to the eastern side of the castle, this flank was then considered less vulnerable to attack. In consequence, the scale of his work here, although formidable, is less elaborate.

From the bridge outside Canon's Gate can be seen the Tudor Bulwark, a rare 16th-century gun platform, projecting into the moat. On the far side, partly shrouded by trees, are the walls of Shoulder of Mutton Battery, constructed in the 1870s as part of new cliff-top defences.

Canon's Gate was built in the mid-1790s to provide a shorter link between the castle and harbour defences than through Constable's Gate. Canon's Gate still has its original two sets of double doors. Immediately inside are casemates built as guardrooms.

Above Canon's Gate, on the left, partly hidden behind the grassy bank, is a brick gunpowder magazine constructed in about 1800. The bank was added about 50 years later as protection from seaward bombardment. Behind it, on the site of the Cinque Ports prison exercise yard, stands the royal garrison artillery barracks,

completed in 1913 for the specialist troops responsible for coastal defence guns. Opposite is the regimental institute, built in 1868 as a canteen and recreation rooms, designed to tempt off-duty soldiers away from the town's taverns. The institute was enlarged later in the 19th century, eventually including a library, reading rooms and a billiard room; similar facilities could be found at military stations throughout the British Empire.

On the ground floor stands one of the most famous artillery pieces in the country. This great bronze gun, popularly known as 'Queen Elizabeth's Pocket Pistol', was cast at Utrecht in 1544 and presented by the emperor Charles V to Henry VIII. It is a 12-pounder brass basilisk, notable for the rich renaissance ornament along its barrel. Towards the breech are two shields, one bearing the English royal arms, the other, nearer the breech, showing the arms of the count of Buren. The gun could fire accurately for up to a mile and a half. It has very probably been at Dover almost continuously since 1545, although it saw service elsewhere in England with both sides during the civil war in the 17th century. The elaborate cast-iron carriage dates from 1827.

North of the regimental institute, the small stone building with its ventilated roof was constructed in 1895 as a bread and meat store. Opposite, the 18th- and 19th-century brick houses against the castle wall incorporate parts of the Cinque Ports prison. More recently they were army married quarters.

Henry III completed the defences from the cliffs to Peverell's Gateway in the 1220s. D-shaped wall towers distinguish his work from that of Henry II, whose engineers favoured rectangular towers. D-shaped towers could better withstand missiles and mining, and were easily covered by fire from adjacent defenders. The surviving fireplace and adjacent latrine at Hurst's Tower shows it was once used as a lodging. Later, many were named after constables, their deputies or lords whose knights served castle-guard (a fixed period of service each year) at Dover. Hurst's, Say's and

Gatton's Towers all have alterations, probably made in about 1800 by Twiss to mount small 12-pounder guns. Outside the curtain wall are the extensive outworks and batteries that Twiss constructed to guard approaches to Canon's Gate.

Peverell's Gate is part of the defences built by King John early in the 13th century. From it, a now-vanished wall extended to the inner bailey near Palace Gate. Originally it had a drawbridge on each side, for better protection. In the 18th century it was briefly used as part of the Cinque Ports prison. Next to it stands an early 19th-century officer's house.

Overlooking Peverell's Gate and the outer curtain are the formidable defences of the 1180s inner bailey, its towers well provided with cross-bow loops. Behind, and dominating everything is the massive keep. Across the valley can be seen the powerful defences of Western Heights. Originally fortified during the American War of Independence (1775–83), these defences were remodelled during the Napoleonic Wars to prevent an enemy encircling the town and harbour from the west.

Left: 'Queen Elizabeth's Pocket Pistol', a 12-pounder brass basilisk [a type of cannon] cast at Utrecht, Holland, in 1544 and presented by the emperor Charles V to Henry VIII. It is known to have been at Dover as early as 1613
Below: Peverell's Gate and the western outer curtain wall, looking north

First floor

Ground floor

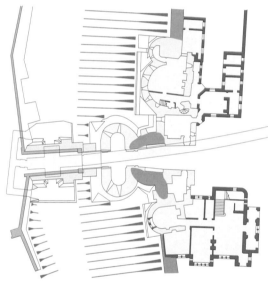

Section

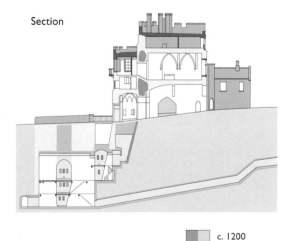

	c. 1200
	1221–30
	1805
	1883
	No visitor access

0 ____ 15 metres

0 ____ 15 yards

North of Peverell's Gate is Constable's Gate, inserted into the curtain wall by Hubert de Burgh between 1221 and 1227 to replace the old north entrance. The core of Constable's Gate is an earlier tower, remodelled with a gate passage and drawbridge. Two D-shaped towers set back-to-back, and two further towers on either side, provided formidable defensive fire. This is one of the most elaborate castle gateways in England, born of the shock of siege and near defeat in 1216.

The constable, who was in charge of the castle, was lodged over the gateway as an added safeguard. Nearly 800 years later, it remains the home of the deputy-constable. The medieval hall partly survives above the archway, but the flanking wings were added in 1883, providing more spacious quarters for a Victorian general. Across the drawbridge is the medieval barbican or defended outwork. This was extensively remodelled during the Napoleonic Wars when a brick caponier was built beneath the bridge to fire along the moat. To guard against bombardment from the north-west, Twiss also constructed the great blunt-ended Constable's Bastion, thrusting out from the hillside to the south-west and mounting four heavy guns. Looking north to the spur, the low concrete parapet and the triple line of concrete anti-tank defences on the western side were added in 1940 as part of defences against a German invasion.

Beyond Constable's Gate, the path passes the 1883 stables and Godsfoe and Crevecoeur Towers in the outer curtain. These towers stand near the site of the king's 'new hall', mentioned in documents in 1214.

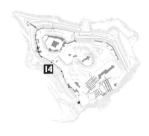

Left: Plans and a cross-section through Constable's Gate, showing the evolution of this powerful defence work from its construction in the 1220s to the final addition of defences in the moat during the Napoleonic wars
Below: A view of Constable's Gate from the north in 1787, showing the then poor condition of the adjacent castle walls

Facing page: The imposing cluster of five towers forming Constable's Gate, constructed after the siege of 1216–17. This was home successively to constables and now to deputy-constables. The windows and brickwork date from later modernizations

⒖ SECRET WARTIME TUNNELS

The first tunnels here were built in the 18th century as underground barracks. During the Second World War, this complex warren of underground rooms and passages was adapted and played a key role during the war. From here, in late May 1940, Admiral Ramsay inspired and directed Operation Dynamo, the Dunkirk evacuation. The tunnels were later adapted to provide secure accommodation for a regional seat of government in the event of a nuclear attack on Great Britain. [The tunnels can be visited by guided tour; the lower levels of the tunnels are not yet open to visitors.]

Casemate Level

The approach to the tunnels is down the sloping access ramp and tunnel cut in 1797. This leads to the terrace outside the main entrance to casemate level and the four large tunnels that were originally soldiers' barracks. East of these, and linked by smaller communication tunnels are a further three large tunnels originally designed as officers' quarters. All were extensively modernized for operations rooms, offices and communications centres in the Second World War and were partially refurbished by the Home Office in the 1960s for canteen use and as sleeping accommodation.

Although the large brick-lined barrack tunnels have been altered and adapted for 20th-century warfare, the narrower communication tunnels remain largely as completed in the early 19th century. Marks of miners' picks are clearly visible in the chalk, while at intervals narrow cylindrical

Facing page: Miners at work extending the cliff tunnels between 1941 and 1943

Above: A painting of 1843 showing troops marching down to the cliff barracks
Left: The exterior of the cliff barracks today

The secret wartime tunnels. This cross-section and plan show the complex network of tunnels developed during and after the Second World War from the original Georgian underground barracks

SECTION LOOKING EAST

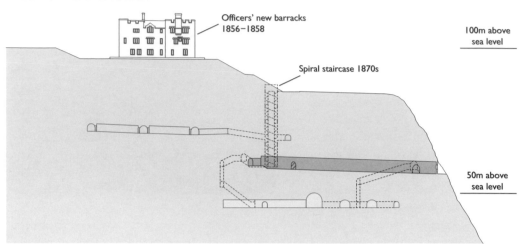

Officers' new barracks 1856–1858

Spiral staircase 1870s

100m above sea level

50m above sea level

PLAN

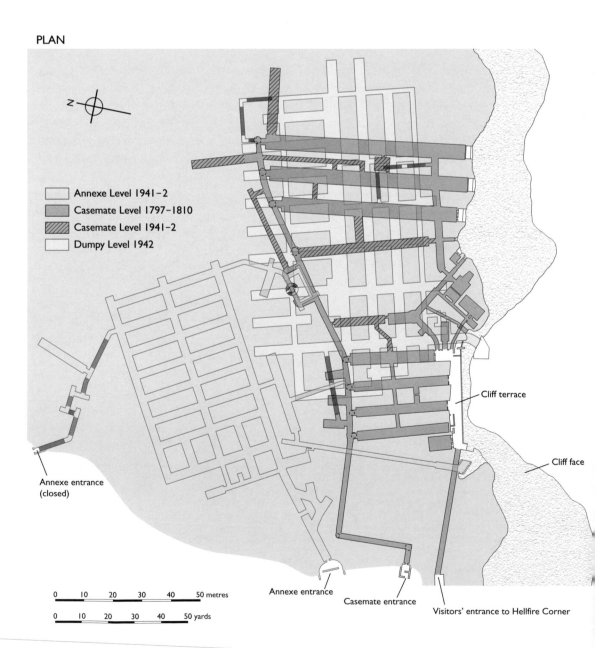

Z

Annexe Level 1941–2
Casemate Level 1797–1810
Casemate Level 1941–2
Dumpy Level 1942

Cliff terrace

Cliff face

Annexe entrance (closed)

Annexe entrance

Casemate entrance

Visitors' entrance to Hellfire Corner

0 10 20 30 40 50 metres

0 10 20 30 40 50 yards

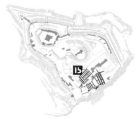

Left: *Part of the reconstructed telephone and telex exchange in the former cliff barracks. The exchange was located here in 1941*

Below: *A wartime photograph of the coastal artillery plotting room. This controlled gun batteries from the North Foreland beyond Ramsgate to Hastings*

shafts rise to the surface for ventilation. Several of the tunnels have had contemporary fittings replaced to give an impression of their appearance in the Second World War. A high proportion of the total space was allocated to communication equipment needed to link the headquarters with the outside world. Telephone lines led directly to the coastal gun batteries, the naval base in Dover harbour, to searchlight positions, anti-aircraft batteries and other military facilities in the area, including the top-secret radar stations. Other lines led to the government in London, to the Admiralty and War Office, as well as to the major naval bases and the main RAF airfields such as Manston, Hawkinge and Biggin Hill. For the Dover headquarters to be effective, it had to be fully informed, to be able to exchange information, as well as to receive and issue orders. The main military telephone exchange, installed here in 1941, has been recreated, using contemporary equipment. This served the entire underground headquarters and was manned around the clock. Adjacent to it, a new tunnel was excavated to contain the huge numbers of batteries and their chargers necessary to keep the telephone equipment working. Nearby, the Navy had radio transmitters and receivers connected to aerials on the surface, allowing

direct communication with naval vessels. Similar equipment linked fast launches stationed to rescue pilots shot down in the Straits.

In 1939, at the outbreak of war, the three main headquarters within the original officers' barracks were the naval headquarters for the Dover command, the coastal artillery operations room and the anti-aircraft operations room.

33

Just over halfway down Admiralty Casemate a doorway leads to a small room excavated in 1942 for the Navy as an operations room and now used to show a short film on Operation Dynamo. This replaced a more cramped space in the main tunnel. Its walls would have been covered with charts and it was here that the senior naval staff directed warships in the Dover command. Relocating the naval operations room here allowed immediate communication with the adjacent coastal artillery operations room, which controlled the harbour guns as well as the coastal artillery. The plotting table displayed here is the original wartime one, but the rest of the display is a reconstruction using mostly original equipment. Further up this tunnel was the anti-aircraft operations room, closely linked to the anti-aircraft gun sites, the searchlight batteries and RAF stations.

In part of the next tunnel is the general post office repeater station. Such repeater stations were needed at approximately 10-mile intervals to amplify telephone messages passing along the land lines. The telephone exchange occupies the far end of this tunnel. A small team of post office engineers was on duty here continuously, to ensure there were no breakdowns. The equipment now here is largely original.

Electrical power for all the lighting and equipment normally came from the mains. However, the uncertainty of wartime supplies led

Left: Winston Churchill emerges from the main wartime entrance to the cliff tunnels during one of his visits to the castle in the Second World War

Below: Vice-Admiral Ramsay's 'cabin' at the end of the Admiralty tunnel during the Second World War. From here, he had a view over the harbour to the Channel beyond. The tape on the windows was to minimize splinters from shell or bomb blasts

Facing page: A reconstruction of part of the anti-aircraft operations room

These last two have been partly reconstructed, using original equipment.

Admiral Ramsay's former naval headquarters remains empty, enabling visitors to appreciate the huge scale of these Georgian underground barracks. In the walls are fireplaces that once warmed George III's officers quartered here, while lines on the walls and on the timber floor, installed in the late 1930s, show where naval office partitions were located. During the war years, this tunnel was a warren of offices, with the admiral's own quarters at the end overlooking Dover harbour and the Straits. Although Ramsay had accommodation in the officers' mess, he also had a bed provided in his staff quarters for use during busy periods. Other staff were not so lucky and in an emergency, as during Operation Dynamo, they had to sleep wherever they could.

Although silent now, little effort of imagination is needed to visualise this once busy hub of naval activity – scene of so many momentous decisions. The route through this tunnel follows the wartime passage that once linked the offices. Above it remains the trunking of the Second World War ventilation system. The cliff front of the tunnel was securely sealed by the Home Office in the 1960s to avoid contamination from nuclear fall-out, at which time the remaining partitions were removed.

Admiral Sir Bertram Home Ramsay (1883–1945)

The extraordinary success of Ramsay's rescue mission at Dunkirk raised British morale at a crucial moment

Admiral Ramsay's pivotal role in organizing the evacuation of the British Expeditionary Force from Dunkirk in late May 1940 saved the core of the British Army from certain defeat and capture by the Germans. Ramsay had joined the Royal Navy as a cadet in January 1898 and had served in the famous Dover patrol from 1915 to the end of the First World War, latterly in command of the destroyer HMS *Broke*. Called back from early retirement at the time of the Munich crisis in 1938, he was appointed a vice-admiral in January 1939 and flag officer, Dover. His task was to ensure the safety of the Straits for Britain and its allies in the event of war with Germany. Ramsay set up his naval headquarters safe from bombing in the eastern of the Georgian tunnels beneath the castle. In May 1940, the lightning advance of Hitler's armies into France had split the British and French forces, leaving the British Army trapped at Dunkirk. The extraordinary success of Ramsay's rescue mission, Operation Dynamo, raised British morale at a crucial moment – the 'Dunkirk spirit' – and allowed the country a vital breathing space.

Ramsay's great skills ensured him a key role in the allied landings later in North Africa and Sicily. In 1944, he masterminded Operation Neptune, the naval side of the D-Day landings in France. As allied naval commander-in-chief for the Normandy invasion, Ramsay was responsible for the biggest and most successful invasion fleet in history. Killed in an air crash in France on 2 January 1945, he was buried with full naval honours at Saint Germain-en-Laye near his headquarters. In a moving tribute, the first lord of the admiralty recorded that 'Admiral Ramsay's courage, drive and skill as an organizer enabled us [at Dunkirk] to retrieve sufficient from the wreck to begin to build again, and to carry on in faith at a time when the world believed that we were defeated.'

Above: A wartime photograph of Vice-Admiral Ramsay in his Dover Castle headquarters

to the installation of an emergency generator for the tunnels. This remains in its own short tunnel at the end of the cliff terrace, by the exit from casemate level.

Annexe Level: the Underground Hospital

The hospital tunnels, known as annexe level, lie above and slightly to the rear of the casemate level tunnels. The main entrance links directly to an ambulance lay-by on the road running up from Canon's Gate. Inside, the differences in plan, scale and construction between the two sets of tunnels are at once apparent. The main tunnels of the 1790s are lofty, spacious chambers, lined with brick. Their 1941 steel-lined successors are far more cramped. The hospital tunnels, unlike their Georgian predecessors, are also laid out on a regular grid pattern.

The hospital was carefully planned as a sequence of reception areas, living quarters, washrooms and latrines, galley and food store, operating theatres and wards. It was designated as a medical dressing station, for dealing with injuries and wounds before patients were transferred to inland hospitals. Although excavated in 1941, the hospital was not fitted out until the following autumn, by which time its size had been scaled down. In part, this was due to fewer casualties in

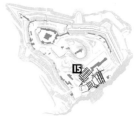

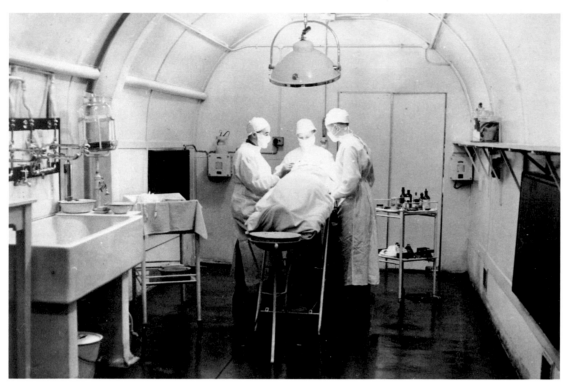

Left: A wartime photograph of the operating theatre in the underground hospital
Below: A wartime photograph of one of the cramped wards in the underground hospital

Facing page: The hospital kitchen in use during the Second World War

the area than anticipated, but mainly to the requirements of the new combined headquarters then being excavated below. The army element of this alone was estimated at 650 officers and men. Although CHQ staff were normally billeted elsewhere in the castle and town, secure sleeping and mess accommodation was needed during times of bombardment or attack. As a result, a substantial part of annexe level was given over to such use from the start. Most of the medical equipment on display is contemporary, and the rooms are based on photographs showing them in use towards the end of the Second World War.

As there were other military and civilian hospitals in and around Dover, the medical dressing station principally served the castle garrison. It was staffed by a full army medical team of surgeons, nurses, orderlies and cooks. Although secure from shelling and bombing, conditions here were not ideal. Lack of any natural light, the constant background noise of the ventilation, and the cramped conditions made life tiring for both staff and patients. However, a medical unit serving the castle garrison continued to be located here into the early 1950s, when these tunnels were abandoned.

During the 1960s, when the regional seat of government was located in the lowest tier of cliff

tunnels, known as Dumpy, annexe level was re-equipped to provide living accommodation. The bunk beds, washroom fittings, latrines and part of the elaborate air-filtration system largely date from this modernization, but differ little from their wartime predecessors.

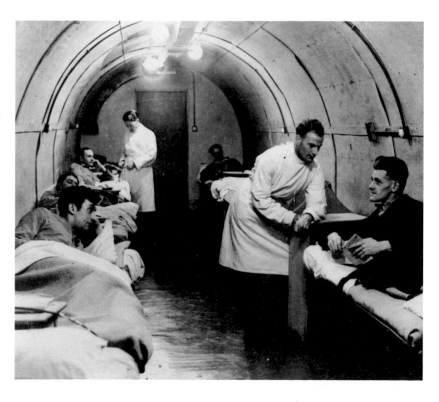

History

Dover's history spans more than nine centuries. William the Conqueror built a castle here in 1066 and it was extended and rebuilt during the medieval period. In 1216 and 1265 the castle withstood two remarkable sieges. By the 18th century, the medieval defences were becoming obsolete, and were adapted for artillery warfare. In the 20th century, the castle again saw active service: during the Second World War, the underground tunnels were the nerve centre for the Dunkirk evacuation; and from the 1960s to the 1980s, the tunnels housed a regional seat of government in case of a nuclear attack.

READING THE HISTORY

This section is arranged chronologically, and describes the history of the castle from the Iron Age to the Cold War.

BEFORE THE CASTLE
An Iron Age Hillfort?

Dover Castle was not the first structure on this windswept hilltop. Medieval military engineers faced with a largely open downland site, as here, would normally have built a castle to a more regular plan. Dover's unusual outline may reflect the reuse and incorporation of an outer ditch and bank from an Iron Age hillfort. Excavations have reputedly found pieces of Iron Age pottery, which would suggest early activity here. The overlapping bank on the eastern side, subsequently protected by Avranches Tower, might have been the site of the main in-turned entrance to an Iron Age fort. Around 50 examples of these hillforts survive in south-east England, where they were used as tribal defences from about the fifth or sixth centuries BC until the Roman invasion of 43 AD. Some were occupied permanently, while others were simply places of refuge.

Facing page: A near-contemporary portrait of Henry II, who built the keep at Dover, from Gerald of Wales's Conquest of Ireland

Below: *Aerial view of Dover Castle from the north, clearly showing its complex layers of defences*

Roman Dover

Immediately after the Roman invasion of Britain in 43 AD, Richborough was developed as the main port in the south-east. Dover was then probably little more than a fishing settlement beside the River Dour. But archaeological excavations by the river have uncovered the remains of a small second-century fort linked to the *Classis Britannica*, the British fleet established by the Romans to guard the coast and the cross-Channel trade routes. Contemporary with this, and further vivid proof of the growing importance of Dover as a port and naval base, is the remarkable *pharos* or lighthouse in the castle. A second lighthouse once stood on Western Heights on the other side of Dover, the two clearly intended to act as beacons, guiding shipping to the port in between. Such lighthouses were then common around the Mediterranean and this pair was almost certainly worked in conjunction with a now-vanished Roman lighthouse, the Tour d'Odre at Boulogne. Unlike modern lighthouses that are identified by the rhythm of their flashing lights, these early ones operated as fire beacons with braziers on their tops providing guiding lights. It is probable that the lighthouse keeper lived beside the lighthouse, but

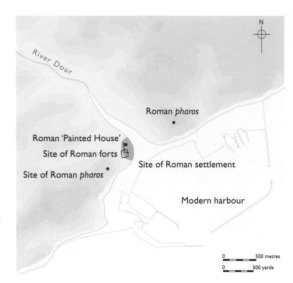

later military works here are likely to have destroyed all traces of any such buildings.

Anglo-Saxon Dover

We know very little of the history of Castle Hill between the Romans' departure early in the fifth century and the construction of the first castle in November 1066, although archaeological investigations have shown that the town of Dover has been continuously inhabited since at least the seventh century. Hilltops without a reliable water

Top right: A map showing the main Roman sites in Dover
Right: A photograph of the ruined church of St Mary-in-Castro before its restoration in 1862. To the right is the Roman lighthouse

Left: The church of St Mary-in-Castro from the north. To its right is the Roman lighthouse partly hidden by the mid-19th-century garrison school. In the foreground, the grassy mound marks the top of the castle well dug in the 1790s. The earthworks to the left of the church are the site of Four-Gun Battery built in the 1750s

Below left: 19th-century engraving and plan of the church and lighthouse

Below: Plans showing the development of Dover Castle, from early settlement to medieval castle

supply are generally unattractive for permanent settlement. However, a seventh-century document mentions a church for 20 canons possibly being founded on this site, although this could refer to the old Roman fort in the valley rather than the presumed abandoned Iron Age hillfort. But the existence here of the late 10th- or early 11th-century church of St Mary-in-Castro, one of the finest Anglo-Saxon churches in Kent, suggests that there was a settlement here at the castle.

Excavations near the church in the 1960s found part of a Saxon cemetery containing graves of men, women and children, indicating an adjacent settlement. This is the best evidence for the existence here of a late Saxon defensive stronghold or burgh. Such communal defences of banked and ditched enclosures were widely constructed during the troubled years of the early 11th century, and it would have been natural to construct one around the church and abandoned lighthouse. This may have developed into a semi-permanent settlement or upper town, a suggestion perhaps reinforced by the account of the fatal brawl in 1051 when Eustace of Boulogne and his men went up to the town and killed more than 20 inhabitants.

Prehistoric earthwork, Roman pharos and Saxon church

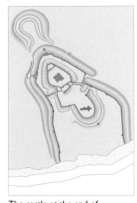

The castle at the end of the 13th century

41

Above: A scene from the Bayeux Tapestry showing the construction of Hastings Castle in 1066. Similar works took place at Dover during William's brief stay here in November following his victory at Hastings

Right: A 13th-century portrait of the great castle-builder Henry II (1154–89), who ordered the rebuilding of Dover Castle in the 1160s

ROYAL CASTLE AND RESIDENCE (1066–1700)

The First Norman Castle

After William the Conqueror's victory at Hastings in 1066, Dover surrendered to his army and he spent eight days constructing fortifications here before advancing to Canterbury. Typically, an early Norman castle had a substantial mound or motte with a timber palisade round the top. At its foot was a large enclosure, or bailey, protected by a ditch and bank, which was topped by another timber palisade. The bailey afforded living space for people and animals and storage room for weapons and provisions, while the motte provided a fighting platform from where archers could command the immediate surroundings.

We know virtually nothing about the first Norman castle at Dover. However, William's very brief stay strongly suggests that he found and strengthened an existing defence, most probably a burgh or banked enclosure round the church and the lighthouse. Limited archaeological evidence has revealed that buried beneath the great 13th-century earthwork that now partly surrounds these is an earlier mid-11th-century bank and ditch. This had been cut through the cemetery, disturbing burials – an act of sacrilege to be understood only in the urgent context of war. These defences, however, proved their worth a year later in 1067, when the garrison beat off

an attack by Count Eustace of Boulogne who had landed to aid the Kentish rebels. The strategic importance of the new castle could not have been more clearly demonstrated.

The Rebuilding of the Castle by Henry II

Little is known about the castle in the century after 1066, until Henry II began the works that by the 1250s had enlarged it into much of its present appearance, transforming it into one of the greatest English medieval fortresses. Contemporaries regarded the king, whose empire stretched from northern England to the Pyrenees, as a famous builder. In England alone, he constructed or modernized about 90 fortifications. Such works mostly cost a few hundred pounds, but recorded expenditure at Dover came to £6,440, greatly in excess of any other castle and a substantial proportion of Henry's income. Clearly, he saw Dover very much as a symbol of royal authority, a frontier fortress overlooking the Straits to the lands of the count of Flanders, a dependent of the king of France.

Work began in the 1160s, but the bulk of expenditure took place between 1179 and 1188

directed by Maurice, one of the greatest contemporary military engineers. His principal works were the great keep and the walls and towers of the inner bailey. But he also began construction of the outer curtain running north from Avranches Tower, following the presumed line of the Iron Age defences. When Henry II died in

1189, the castle must have been a vast construction site, with most of the labour force, as recent excavations have suggested, living in the developing St James's district of Dover at the foot of the hill. When completed by his successors, it became the first castle in western Europe with concentric layers of defences encircling the keep at its heart.

Left: The keep from the north-west

Above: French troops attack the northern defences of the castle during the siege of 1216. This reconstruction drawing shows the scene viewed from the top of the keep

Below right: The battle of Sandwich Bay in August 1217. Hubert de Burgh's ships defeated French reinforcements, ending all hopes of a French victory on land

Facing page: King John, from an early 14th-century manuscript. John's building work at Dover was crucial in enabling the castle to withstand the great siege at the end of his reign

The Great Siege and Completion of the Castle (1189–1250)

Following the loss of Normandy in 1204, King John pressed ahead with finishing the outer curtain wall. His engineers designed a series of D-shaped towers that can be followed from the north-east side, anti-clockwise round to Peverell's Tower. A now-vanished length of wall joined Peverell's Tower to the inner bailey near Palace Gate, while the main outer gateway was constructed at the northern tip of the castle. This work must have been finished when the castle withstood its famous siege in the civil war between King John and the barons.

The king barely had time to provision the castle in May 1216 and install 140 knights under Hubert de Burgh, justiciar of England, before it was besieged by French forces commanded by Prince Louis, who were aiding the rebels. By the autumn, only Windsor and Dover Castles remained in the king's hands in southern England.

Prince Louis established his main siege camp on higher ground just north of the castle. From here, great stone-throwing engines bombarded the walls, while miners tunnelled underneath the northern barbican. Only when the barbican partly collapsed did the spirited garrison cease their sorties and withdraw behind the north gateway.

Resuming work, the French miners next attacked the eastern gate tower. Surviving tunnels here may well be countermines dug unsuccessfully by the garrison hoping to intercept the miners. As the French poured over the collapsed tower, Hubert's knights engaged them in bitter hand-to-hand fighting, finally driving them back.

This assault was the climax. A truce followed that lasted until May 1217 when Louis resumed the siege, but the battle of Lincoln ended rebel hopes. Dover Castle, after a year of sieges and truces, remained uncaptured although badly damaged.

The siege had dramatically exposed the weakness of the castle's northern defences. Work to remedy this and complete the outer curtain walls was to extend over the next 30 years of Henry III's reign. Soon after the siege, Hubert de Burgh had the northern gateway blocked solid. Beyond, in the moat, engineers constructed St John's Tower, while beyond that the ruined northern barbican was replaced by a new outwork or spur, to give the garrison a better command of the high ground to the north. Tower and spur were linked to the castle by a tunnel and drawbridge. The formidably strong Constable's Gate with its cluster of six towers was built on the western side of the castle as the new main entrance, while Fitzwilliam Gate was inserted as a secondary entrance on the eastern side (see plan on inside back cover).

Elsewhere, the outer curtain walls were extended to the cliff edge, finally completing the work begun by Maurice some 40 years earlier. The massive bank to the south of the church and lighthouse was also constructed and its timber palisade replaced by a stone wall in 1256. Dover Castle had now reached the zenith of its medieval might. A few years later, in 1265, the castle was again besieged when it was held by Simon de Montfort's widow, Eleanor, during the baronial revolt (see page 14). In an unexpected twist of fate, royalist prisoners helped overthrow the garrison and the castle suffered little damage.

Hubert de Burgh

Hubert de Burgh, whose leadership saved Dover during the great siege of 1216–17, was undoubtedly brave, but also ruthless, able and ambitious. Born in Norfolk, he joined the court as a young man, probably in the 1190s, eventually running the future King John's household as his chamberlain. In 1201 King John granted him the castles of Grosmont, Skenfrith and Whitecastle on the Welsh borders; he was later to acquire further castles. He first gained fame for his stubborn if unsuccessful year-long defence of the great castle of Chinon against the French king in 1204–5. Ten years later John appointed him as justiciar, the country's chief legal officer, able to deputize for the monarch. His legendary defence of Dover was followed in August 1217 by victory in the naval battle off Sandwich, the first of a series between England and France. The chronicler Matthew Paris recorded that before the battle Hubert told his men that, if he were captured, they should allow his execution rather than surrender the castle, 'for it is the key to England'. From 1217 to 1221 he personally supervised the strengthening of Dover Castle before delegating its completion to trusted assistants. To pay for this and for the garrison, Hubert used the Kent 'scutage' or money payments in place of castle-guard, as well as the entire revenues of the counties of Norfolk, Suffolk and Kent, where he was sheriff. He also began construction of Hadleigh Castle overlooking the Thames estuary. In 1221, he had married his fourth wife, Margaret, sister of King Alexander of Scotland. Throughout the 1220s he retained his position as justiciar, effectively in charge of the administration of the country during a time of turbulence and political intrigue. In 1227, Henry III came of age. That year, Hubert was created earl of Kent, but in 1232 he lost the support of the young king. Stripped of office and of the castles granted to him, he was briefly imprisoned. Although his own lands were restored to him and he was later reconciled with Henry III, he retired from public life and died in 1243.

Hubert told his men that if he were captured, they should allow his execution rather than surrender the castle, 'for it is the key to England'

Above: Hubert de Burgh kneels at an altar

Life in Medieval Dover

Castle carpenters constructed a house for 'Gerard the Crossbowman'

In peacetime, there may have been a dozen knights resident at Dover, together with some foot-soldiers, warders and porters. Provision of these relied on the system of castle-guard, where larger baronial estates annually provided a knight for 40 days' service. This was neither popular nor efficient. After the 1216 siege, service was replaced by a money payment, allowing establishment of a permanent and more experienced garrison.

The constable, first appointed by King Stephen (1135–54) was in charge of the castle and its garrison and was responsible for entertaining numerous important visitors from the monarch downwards. A century later, his duties were combined with those of lord warden of the Cinque Ports Confederation. This had been established in the 11th century, when the five port towns of Sandwich, Dover, Hythe, Romney and Hastings had promised to provide ships and men to defend the coast and protect shipping. These ports were later joined by others, attracted by privileges that included their own courts of justice and immunity from national taxation. The lord warden was created to control the confederation and act as a link with the government. He was responsible for coastal defences locally, overseeing Channel shipping and providing ships from the Cinque Ports at the king's command. His task was helped by appointment of a deputy-constable at Dover, responsible for the castle.

Accommodation here varied. The keep was used occasionally when the court visited, but its layout was inconvenient and its main function outside war was probably for ceremonial purposes. Records show it mostly standing empty. King John had a great hall and chamber built in the inner bailey; this was replaced by the partly surviving Arthur's Hall in 1240. From 1227, the constable lived in Constable's Tower. There are references to thatched houses near the church, granaries, ovens and at least two windmills for grinding corn, and to castle carpenters constructing a house for 'Gerard the Crossbowman'.

Above: A medieval soldier with a crossbow. Although this weapon was greatly feared, the time taken to tension the bow by means of its windlass meant that its rate of fire was slow
Right: A reconstruction drawing of Dover Castle at the height of its medieval development in the middle of the 13th century

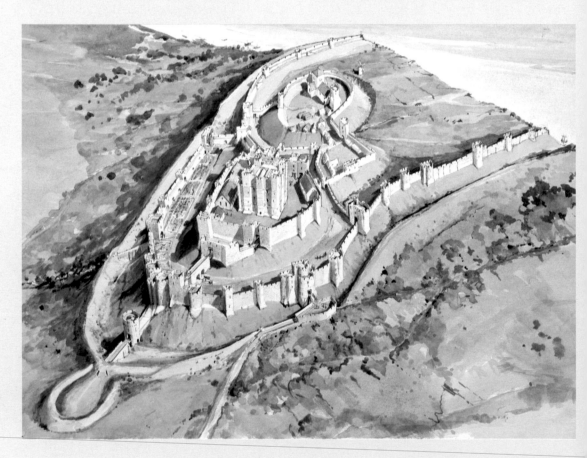

The Castle's Changing Role

The castle remained garrisoned during the 15th century, serving as the administrative centre for the Cinque Ports and a convenient lodging for important travellers waiting to cross the Channel. In the late 15th century, the keep was modernized with new windows, doorways and fireplaces, but its military architecture was not easily adapted to changing tastes. In 1624, its interior was elaborately refurbished for Henrietta Maria of France on her way to marry the future Charles I. Her disgruntled chamberlain recorded that she was badly lodged in poor accommodation. The keep was never used again as a royal residence.

But Dover's military role had declined long before. Effective ordnance introduced late in the 15th century made most medieval defences obsolete. Henry VIII's artillery forts of the late 1530s, such as Deal and Walmer Castles, were a radical new design, built by the shore to fire at approaching ships. At Dover, the contemporary Moat's Bulwark and Archcliffe Fort were similarly sited. Almost as a token, the castle was given a few guns, mounted near the cliff edge or possibly on the tiny gun platform outside the later Canon's Gate.

In 1642, on the outbreak of the Civil War, the small royalist garrison was captured after a body of townsmen daringly scaled the cliffs. But this was more symbolic than of practical consequence and its apparent obsolescence probably saved the castle from being slighted. In the 1680s, the keep briefly held prisoners-of-war, but the castle was described as 'ruinous' and in 1708 the lord warden moved to Walmer Castle.

Top: A 16th-century view of Dover from the sea by Anthonis Wyngaerde
Above: Henrietta Maria, wife of Charles I. Her entourage was not impressed with accommodation in the castle in 1624
Below: Wenceslaus Hollar's engraving of the castle in 1645 from Western Heights. Prominent in the foreground are the ruins of the second Roman lighthouse

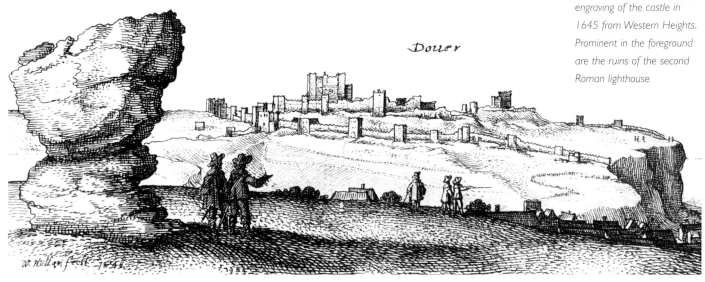

Above: Part of the castle and harbour from a painting of 1825 by J M W Turner
Below: The first duke of Dorset returning to the castle in a procession after taking the oath of office as lord warden in 1727. This oil painting by John Wootton clearly shows how the harbour was then largely located west of the town

A GARRISON FORTRESS (1700–1850)

From the 1740s, the castle's decline was abruptly reversed. By then, any invading armies needed to capture a port to unload heavy artillery. Dover harbour's proximity to Europe made it highly vulnerable, despite protection from the surviving Tudor Moat's Bulwark and Archcliffe Fort below Western Heights. The government now feared a swift overland attack to capture the harbour by enemy infantry landed near Walmer or Hythe, so the castle had a vital defensive role.

In 1744, when a Jacobite invasion from Dunkirk threatened, new barracks were built in the inner bailey, followed ten years later by remodelled troop accommodation in the keep. The military engineer J P Desmaretz also reformed the northern defences from Avranches Tower to the Norfolk Towers for heavy artillery and constructed Bell Battery and Four-Gun Battery. These gun positions covered the high ground to the north-east, marking the first major additions to the castle's defences for 500 years.

Even more spectacular developments were completed during the wars with France between 1793 and 1815. The military engineer William Twiss totally remodelled the outer defences, adding the massive Horseshoe, Hudson's, East Arrow, East Demi- and Constable's Bastions to augment fire-power on the eastern side and western sides. To strengthen the northern tip of the castle he reformed the spur, adding a redan or raised artillery platform. Canon's Gate was also built to speed troop movements between castle and town.

Within the castle, Twiss stripped the roof from the keep and replaced it with massive brick vaults to support heavy artillery on the top. Housing soldiers to man the new defences presented major problems because of lack of space for more barracks and in 1797 a revolutionary solution was adopted. The Royal Engineers brought in a company of miners to start excavating a series of seven parallel tunnels as barracks running in from the cliff face some 15m (50ft) below the cliff top. These were linked at the rear by a communication passage and were provided with fireplaces, sanitation and a well. Four tunnels were for soldiers, with three for officers. The first troops moved in during 1803. At their peak in the Napoleonic Wars, the tunnels accommodated more than 2000 men in total security. They are the only underground barracks ever built in Great Britain.

Beyond the town, Twiss was also busy building defences on Western Heights – the largest fortifications built in Britain during the Napoleonic Wars. The addition of these ensured that Dover now had its two most vulnerable landward approaches well defended. All these works were at their height during the crucial years from 1803 to 1805, when a French invasion was expected daily, and town and castle were packed with troops.

After 1815, the underground tunnels were partly used by the coast blockade service, set up

to combat smuggling gangs. But the murder of a quartermaster on the beach below in 1826 led to the headquarters being relocated closer to the shore. For over a century, the tunnels remained largely abandoned.

Above: Looking south from the Norfolk Towers to King's Gate and its barbican with the keep beyond, as recorded in the 1840s

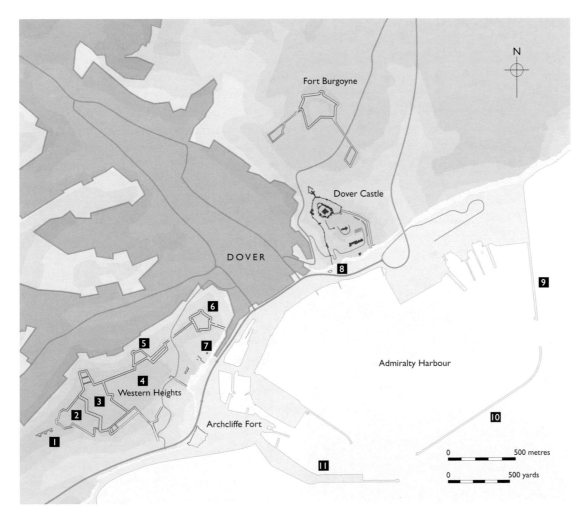

A map showing Western Heights and the later defences of Dover

1 Citadel Battery
2 Western Outworks
3 The Citadel
4 Parade Ground
5 North Centre Bastion
6 Drop Redoubt
7 Grand Shaft
8 Moat's Bulwark
9 Eastern Arm
10 Southern Breakwater
11 Admiralty Pier

Above: The rescue of the British Army from Dunkirk at the end of May 1940. Charles Cundall's dramatic painting of the scene off the beaches

Below: On 1 July 1940, nine days after the French armistice, Herman Goering [sixth from right] and senior German officers look across the Straits to a Britain preparing for a German invasion

Facing page: Churchill and Ramsay confer in the Admiralty tunnel

ADAPTING TO MODERN WARFARE (1850–1984)

Improvements for the Garrison

Following the Napoleonic Wars, little was done to the castle's defences until the 1850s, when the inner bailey gateways and wall-walks were remodelled. However, new and vastly more powerful guns then being introduced were rapidly ending the castle's days as a major fortress. In 1860, the castle was effectively replaced by the construction of Fort Burgoyne just to the north. The castle, however, had a continuing use as a garrison headquarters. From the 1850s to the 1930s, barracks continued to be built here, including Salvin's officers' new barracks of 1858, that still dominate the southern part of the castle. The ruined St Mary-in-Castro

was restored as the garrison church by Sir George Gilbert Scott in 1862. The last major re-arming in the 19th century was the cliff-top gun positions installed in the 1870s to protect the harbour.

In the Eye of the Storm: the Castle in the 20th Century

At the end of the 19th century, the great outer breakwaters of Dover harbour were constructed to provide a secure anchorage for the Royal Navy. This was to revive a naval link with the castle that had lapsed in the 15th century, when the Cinque Ports had ceased to provide ships for royal service. Gun batteries ringed the new Admiralty Harbour, with emplacements on the central breakwater and Western Heights. Advances in fire control allowed all these to be centrally co-ordinated from the castle and in 1905 the obsolete 1870s Hospital Battery on the cliff edge was adapted as a fire command post. In 1914, the Admiralty's port war signal station that controlled all shipping entering and leaving the harbour was located immediately overhead. During the First World War, the castle accommodated a variety of units, including naval crews manning the first anti-aircraft searchlights. For many soldiers returning from the western battlefields, the castle retained its symbolic importance. In a speech in the town in 1918, Field Marshal Lord Haigh declared that, 'the sight of the cliffs of Dover, and the great castle crowning

them, with our empire's flag – the worldwide emblem of freedom for which we have fought – is a most inspiring spectacle, and itself repays us for all that we have been privileged to do in the discharge of our duty to our king and country'.

In 1938, with war again looming, Dover command naval headquarters, the fortress commander and the coastal and anti-aircraft command centres were all located safe from air attack in adjacent tunnels in the old Napoleonic cliff barracks under the castle. Coastal guns from Hastings to the North Foreland were controlled from here. Here too, in late May 1940, Vice-Admiral Ramsay organized, directed and inspired the rescue of the British Expeditionary Force and units of the French army from the harbour and beaches of Dunkirk. At the start of the evacuation on 26 May it was thought 45,000 men might be saved. Despite heavy casualties, when it finished eight day later, ships of the Royal Navy and merchant marine, aided by an armada of small craft largely manned by volunteers, had rescued over 338,000 troops. Britain's chances of survival had been given an incalculable boost. Dover Castle was once again on the front line, a witness that summer to British convoys being doggedly fought through the Straits of Dover and the Battle of Britain raging overhead. Cross-Channel guns provided an additional hazard, giving this part of Kent the title 'Hellfire Corner'. The castle itself suffered bombing and was provisioned to withstand a six-week siege if the Germans invaded; mercifully, Hitler never attempted Operation Sealion – the German code-name for the invasion of Britain.

From June 1940, Dover Castle, now faced German-occupied France and throughout that

Working in Wartime Dover Castle

Mary Horsfall joined the WRNS [Women's Royal Naval Service] at the age of 20 in December 1941 as a signals/watch-keeper and a few weeks later was posted to Vice-Admiral Ramsay's staff in the tunnels under the castle. In 1988, she was asked about her experiences here. She recalled that strict wartime security meant that she could not tell anyone where she was. After her arrival, she said:

'I rang my mother and said, "The castle is just as wonderful as I always knew it would be," and she knew that all my life Dover Castle had meant something to me… and she put two and two together and she knew I was in Dover.'

Mary's feelings for the castle were shared by many wartime service people:

'Suddenly here you are, confronted with Dover Castle, which is so tremendously strong, wonderfully British, wonderfully English. It's been there, it's stuck it out all that time and nothing is ever going to change that and I think that made a profound impression on us [the naval staff and garrison], and I think when things started to go wrong, the fact that Dover Castle was Dover Castle as it looked all chunky and tremendous, it held everything together. I don't think we talked about it, but I think we all felt it'.

On one of Churchill's visits to the naval operations room, he asked Mary if she was frightened when the German cross-Channel guns were shelling Dover:

'I couldn't quite believe that this man was asking me this question. And I stood in front of him and I burst out laughing and I said, "Good gracious, no sir," laughing, and I got into terrible trouble for having laughed at the Prime Minister. But it came from the heart, it had never entered our heads, it was part of the job. There was no fear, no nothing attached to it at all.'

Suddenly here you are, confronted with Dover Castle, which is so tremendously strong, wonderfully British

Above: Mary Horsfall as a Third Officer WRNS, October 1943

summer daily expected invasion. Garrison numbers soared as troops and defence works were poured into Kent. Long-range guns were installed to shell enemy shipping and gun batteries on the coast opposite. By 1943, the Dover garrison alone numbered 10,500 troops. As the military build-up continued, expansion of the underground headquarters became essential.

In 1941, an underground hospital, code-named Annexe, was excavated higher in the cliff. Attempts to tunnel behind the existing headquarters had to be abandoned because of geological faults. However, in March 1942, the War Cabinet ordered further expansion of the tunnel system in case it was needed as a forward combined headquarters for the projected invasion of Europe. A new grid of tunnels was excavated below the two existing layers and completed in mid-1943. Code-named Dumpy, it augmented and to some extent replaced the headquarters function of the original 18th-century tunnels, known as Casemate. Dover was matched by similar installations near Portsmouth and Plymouth. It remained fully operational until victory in 1945. For a few years, the Army and Navy retained some facilities here, including a medical centre, but by the early 1950s the Dover tunnels had been abandoned and in 1958 the castle garrison was finally withdrawn.

In the early 1960s, the abandoned tunnels were secretly equipped and modernized to serve as a regional seat of government following a nuclear attack, which it was assumed would have destroyed London and most of central government. The Cuban missile crisis of 1962, which brought the world to the brink of nuclear war, gave added urgency to the task. Under the control of a minister or regional commissioner, these seats of government were to provide the policy-making framework within their regions to help to re-establish a semblance of normal life. The tunnels now had to be adapted to cope with nuclear contamination and to provide radiation-proof living quarters for about 270 people. These were drawn from government ministries, local authorities, the armed services and the BBC. All might have to remain underground for weeks until radiation levels dropped. Elaborate air-filtering machinery, a huge new generator with its oil-storage tanks, substantial food stores, secure water supplies and communications equipment were installed, together with kitchens and dormitories, and external openings were sealed. A small BBC studio here was to instruct and inform the surviving population. Regular secret exercises was held, but in the early 1980s, the labyrinth of tunnels was found to be inefficient and too costly to run. The whole complex remained on the Secret List until abandoned in 1984.

Above top: The equipment of the Cold War: a Russian alphabet typewriter
Above middle: A 1960s contamination monitor made by Plessey Nucleonics to measure radioactivity after a nuclear attack
Above: A 1980 booklet issued by the Home Office on how to survive a nuclear attack
Right: An exercise in a regional seat of government
Far right: Dover Castle on a 1974 Soviet army map. The Russians prepared maps of 103 British towns and cities for use during an invasion

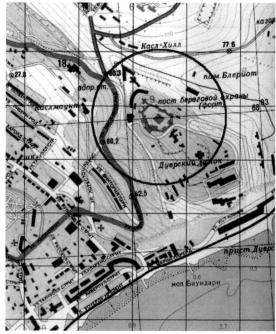